painting with
WATERCOLOURS

Watercolour illustrations by Peter Wilks and Diana Morice
Written by Hal Norman

imagine THAT!™

Imagine That! is an imprint of Top That! Publishing plc,
Tide Mill Way, Woodbridge, Suffolk, IP12 IAP, UK
www.topthatpublishing.com
Copyright © 2004 Top That! Publishing plc
Imagine That! is a trademark of Top That! Publishing plc
All rights reserved

Contents

Introduction

The great thing about watercolour painting is that not only is it an accessible art form, it is a challenging one as well. While the serious artist will always find it testing, the novice will quickly be able to gain an impressive degree of competence. What is more, it is not a daunting hobby to take up as it is quick, clean and portable.

The translucent, light quality of watercolours can be used to create beautiful effects and help to make it one of the most expressive of art forms. Watercolour painting is also exciting because you can veer from loosely controlled strokes to intricate precision within the course of a single painting.

The first few pages of this book contain all you need to get the most out of your materials and should enable you to enjoy completing the projects which follow.

Materials and Equipment

The vital tools for watercolour painting are a sketchpad, paints, brushes, a water container, a mixing palette, a board, a pencil, watercolour paper, tissue and a putty eraser.

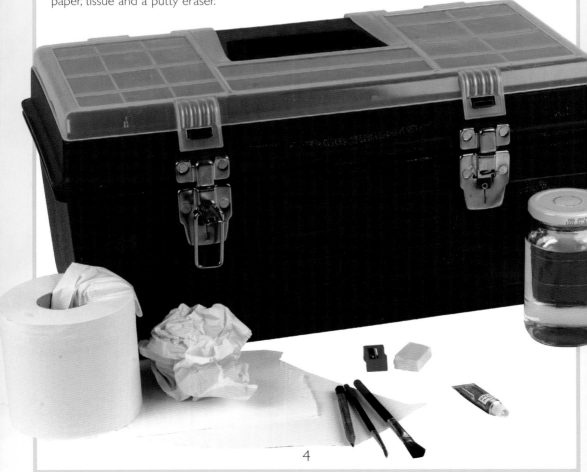

Paints

There are two types of watercolour paints available: student quality and artist quality. Student-quality paints are fine for the beginner and even the intermediate artist but they do not have the same quality of pigment as required by the serious artist.

The paints are available in pans or tubes of varying sizes. Tubes are more convenient when painting large areas as they cause less wear to brushes and save time. Pans, which come in either small, square blocks or larger, rectangular blocks are smaller and easier to transport. There is no need to stick to a particular brand of paint as the paints should be compatible regardless of manufacturer.

Brushes

There is a wide variety of brushes available. The differences are in cost, the amount of water they hold, the ability to maintain a sharp point and the effects they create. There are round brushes, flat brushes, riggers for producing long fine lines, fan brushes for special effects and wash brushes for applying large areas of colour.

Unsurprisingly, perhaps, the best brushes will also be the most expensive. However, bear in mind that the beginner only needs a few brushes. Investment in sable brushes should also prove economically prudent in the long run – as long as the brushes are looked after – and will make it easier for you to establish a degree of control and spontaneity over your work.

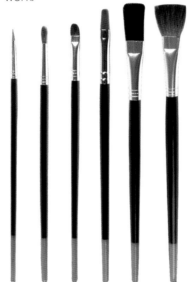

Having said that, there are some fine quality synthetic brushes available that offer a realistic alternative to sable. They can last for a good length of time and are considerably cheaper.

Mixing Palette

Palettes are available in metal, plastic and porcelain. It must be white, so that the colours can be seen clearly and it should have a number of mixing wells with sufficient depth to allow mixing of a number of separate washes. It is easier to gauge the intensity of colour in a flat-well palette than in a slanted-well palette. Many people use ordinary household plates.

Cartridge paper.

Paper

It's worth investing in some good-quality watercolour paper once you have practised a lot and are comfortable with your paints. There are three types of paper available: hot-pressed, cold-pressed and rough. Hot-pressed is good for paintings requiring fine control, cold-pressed is fine for most techniques and rough suits dry-brush techniques. Rough paper will also withstand a lot of wetting and scratching out.

You may find it beneficial to experiment with different papers to find out what suits you best but, when starting out, it makes sense to start with a standard 300 gsm paper.

Watercolour paper. Good-quality watercolour has more texture than cartridge paper.

It's worth noting that you may get away with not stretching thick stock paper and that the lighter grades are liable to bubble when wet.

Pencil

Use a soft pencil to lightly sketch out the composition of your subject before you begin to use your paints. With practice, you will be able to draw with your brush but, to begin with, it helps to work to a pencil-sketched piece, however vague.

Putty Eraser

Keep a soft eraser close at hand to rub out any visible lines once your paint has dried. Unlike a conventional eraser a putty eraser used gently will not damage paper unduly and will allow further paint application. Fashion the putty eraser into a fine point when you want to erase a small area.

Sketchpad

A sketchpad is immensely useful but only if used in a way that is effective. Ideally, you should do several sketches of your subject on your sketchpad, testing different designs and compositions, then progress to delicate sketches on watercolour paper before beginning to paint over the top of this fine pencil work.

Use the sketchpad to capture specific details of your composition, such as small objects and people, for reference.

Do not be tempted to skip the sketchpad section as this may have a detrimental effect on the quality of your work.

7

Setting Up

As with so many things in life, preparation is vital. The following list represents the best practice method:

Location

Before you begin painting scour your location carefully. You might be in an attractive spot but the angle at which you paint your subject can make a big difference. When painting, look at your subject frequently, to see how shadow and light are affecting your work. Also, if painting still life, check that you have positioned the objects within your painting correctly.

Equipment

It may sound obvious but before you start painting make sure you have all the tools you're going to need within easy reach.

Preparing the Surface

Always support your work with an improvised or shop-bought drawing board. Secure your sketching paper with masking tape, or for final pieces, stretch your watercolour paper (see page 10).

Sketches

Do lots of pencil sketches first, building confidence in your skills. Your last sketch should be on the same paper you wish to paint on. Keep pencil lines soft and delicate.

Paint

Always mix more paint than you need. When applying washes make sure all your colours are ready mixed and keep the brush full and watery.

Water

Keep water to hand, in an old coffee or jam jar. Clean water will enable you to produce pure colour mixes. If painting on location outside you will need more water than can be contained in a jar so take a reserve supply.

Other Equipment

You will need some tissue or rag to hand, to lift off wrongly placed colour. Sponges can be used for creating textures and wetting areas. If painting outside in bright conditions, consider sporting a peaked hat. Sitting in the sun for hours can place a strain on your eyes.

Basics

Warm to cool.

Stretching Paper

Watercolour paper should be stretched prior to painting to prevent it cockling (wrinkling and bending). Wet the paper, then fasten the edges of the paper to a board with moistened paper tape (available from artists' shops). Leave to dry completely. The resulting paper is stretched like a drum.

Cool to warm.

Cool and Warm Colours

Colours are divided into two groups: warm and cool. Red, orange and yellow are warm, blue and green are cool. Colours can be warmed up, or cooled down, by adding a little of a colour from the opposite group. The effect will depend on the proportion of each colour used.

How to Hold a Brush

Your hand should be comfortable when you paint, or your work will look strained and stiff. Hold your brush in the middle between your thumb and forefinger, and practise making a few strokes in the air before you load it with paint or water. If you want greater control over your brush – particularly useful when painting fine details – hold the brush a little nearer the bristles.

Light and Shade

The more paint you use, the less light will be present within your picture. The purest colours are made by combining two primary colours. Nature, however, rarely produces these hues; light and shadow have the effect of brightening or dulling a colour. You can show this by using greys, browns and purples to represent areas of shadow and distinguishing highlights.

MIXING PALETTE

The colour block below shows you which colours you need to combine, with water, to create different shades of paint. Practise mixing on a palette before painting a picture. For large areas of colour, mix plenty of colour first, as it is hard to recreate an exact shade.

	Crimson Red	Burnt Sienna	Yellow Ochre	Lemon Yellow	Deep Green	Ultra Marine	Prussian Blue
Crimson Red							
Burnt Sienna							
Yellow Ochre							
Lemon Yellow							
Deep Green							
Ultra Marine							
Prussian Blue							

Washes

Flat Wash

A flat wash is simply a wash of the same colour tone. Use the biggest brush you can and keep a good mixture of paint and water ready. Paint from the top in horizontal, slightly zigzag strokes, keeping within marked boundaries outlined in pencil, and let each stroke settle before continuing. Remove excess fluid with the tip of a dry brush.

Graduated Wash

A graduated, or graded wash, can be either a wash with changes in the intensity of colour, or a wash which changes from one colour to another. The two principle graduated washes are grading from dark to light and grading from one colour to another.

Grading from Dark to Light

Start with full colour at the top and add more and more water as you move down the page. The effect is translucent and allows the texture of the paper to show through.

Grading from One Colour to Another

Instead of diluting the first paint colour, simply add more and more of the new colour. Mix the two different pigment solutions before you start, then make a broad stroke with one. Follow this with a blend of the two colours, and then finish with a brush dipped in only the second colour.

Blended Wash

A blended wash begins in the graded manner. The brush is then rinsed, loaded with a contrasting colour and stroked across the top of the graded area, blending in with it.

Variegated Wash

A variegated wash is a wash of several different colours in either a deliberate or a haphazard way. The colours are allowed to bleed into each other. This wash can work particularly well when painting sunsets.

Techniques

Solid shading

Solid shading is used to create strong contrast between the light and dark areas of a picture. For this to be effective, you should use complementary colours in the lighter areas of the painting.

Highlights

A small, soft ball of tissue can be used to blot wet washes into cloud shapes and add softly highlighted areas. The effect here has been achieved by gently dabbing a ball of tissue over long, thin areas of damp paint, removing the colour and leaving soft edges to look like clouds. In some places, a little paint has been allowed to remain, creating areas of highlight.

Hatching

Hatching is used to darken one side of an object, throwing it into shade. This effect is created by using lots of thin, closely-packed lines along the area in shadow. It's important not to overuse this technique as you may end up with a picture that looks laboured.

14

Crosshatching

Crosshatching allows you to depict shadow on curves and rounded objects. This effect is created by crisscrossing lines to create an area of raised shadow. As with hatching, this technique should be used sparingly and only for special effect.

Wet-in-Wet

Wet-in-wet just means applying paint to wet paper or a colour which is still wet. The wet-in-wet technique can be applied over existing washes provided they are dry. Simply wet the paper with a large brush and paint into the dampness. The soft marks will work well in subtle background areas.

Dry Brush

Load a brush with paint (and very little water) and drag it over bone-dry paper. The marks produced by this technique work best around a painting's focal point as they are crisp and hard edged. This is another technique to be used sparingly and with care.

Textures

Masking Fluid

Masking fluid can be removed and used to create highlights in compositions. Apply to your paper and allow to dry thoroughly. Subsequent washes of paint will simply slide off.

Salt

Scattering salt crystals into wet paint can make for some interesting effects. Lay down a wash, scatter the salt crystals, then leave the wash to dry completely before gently brushing the salt.

Soap

Mixing paint with soap can create some interesting, if unpredictable, results. Soap will thicken paint without affecting its translucency.

Sponge

Dabbing paint onto paper with sponges over washes creates great effects but don't overdo it. Sponges can be used to suggest ripples on water and even for hair.

Stippling

Load a small amount of paint onto an old brush or sponge and then 'pounce' up and down on the paint surface. This will allow some of the background colour to show through, adding texture to your painting.

Toned Ground

A toned ground is simply a base colour which is flooded and allowed to dry. The painting is then painted on top of the base colour. This effect can be used to create a mood for a painting.

Line and Wash

Line and wash can be approached in two ways. Start with a line pen drawing (any water-soluble pen will do) and work water into and over the drawing. This can give very satisfactory results and, with the addition of a few colours, is a good way to start some projects. Alternatively, start with a watercolour wash and while it is still wet, draw into it with pen and ink. This will create some interesting effects but bear in mind that different inks will make for different effects.

Perspective

The most important thing to remember is that figures appear smaller as they get further away from the viewer. Also, they usually become less detailed and softer in tone and colour.

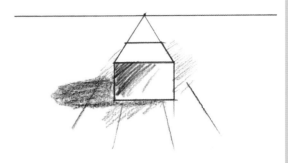

1. An object can be drawn with all the lines disappearing to one point – the vanishing point. The vanishing point sits on the horizon line – the line at which the sky and sea appear to meet.

2. Here the eye level is above the top of the object, so the object is looked down upon. The perspective lines disappear into two vanishing points.

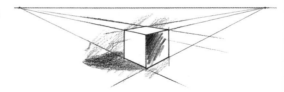

3. In this view the eye level is near the middle of the object. Painting at this level creates the impression that the subject is at the same level as the artist.

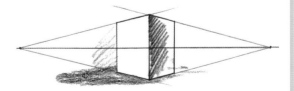

18

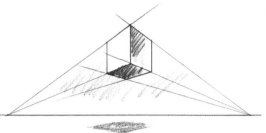

4. Here the eye level is below the object. Bear in mind what response the angle at which the subject is painted may inspire in the viewer. The viewer will undoubtedly respond differently to two paintings of the same subject from different angles.

5. In this sketch, the viewer's eye level is at the same level as the figure in the picture. This creates an interesting effect, perhaps providing a sense of realism in the sketch.

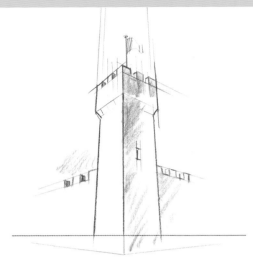

6. Add drama to tall buildings by using two vanishing points as before but this time add a third vanishing point, for the building to disappear into. To help the effect, eye level should be at the base of the object being drawn. The angle at which you paint a building is particularly important. From a straight-on perspective, it will look flat and one-dimensional.

7. When drawing cylindrical or unusual shapes using straight lines will ensure that you get it right. Here, two diagonal lines disappearing to two vanishing points establish the centre line in this perspective. An ellipse can then be drawn in the square.

8. By establishing the first ellipse you can then chart the position of the second. The ellipses effectively sit in a box. The lines of the box can be erased at a later stage.

9. To draw a vase or similar object, draw
   ellipses in perspective around a centre line
   to make the shape symmetrical. The
   simplest way to draw an ellipse is to draw
   a rectangle first and then draw an ellipse
   touching the sides afterwards.

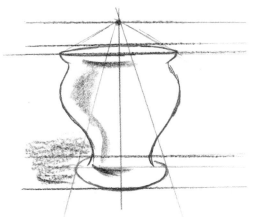

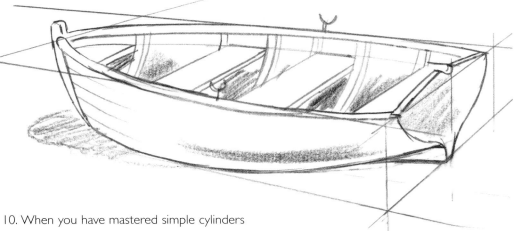

10. When you have mastered simple cylinders
    and vases you can move onto more
    complex items, such as fishing boats. Once
    again, use a perspective box to help you
    draw the shape. The lines disappear in the
    same way as before.

Basic Landscape

When painting landscape scenes there is no need to pick a complex subject. A relatively sparse landscape can be more attractive than one with many focal points fighting for attention.

1. Sketch or trace the line drawing on page 58. Use the sketch opposite to establish tonal values. Pencil in the main shapes, making sure you are aware of where the light is coming from and where the highlights will fall on your subject.

2. Wash in the sky areas with different shades of blue. When painting sky, start with the darkest blue, so that the colour gradually fades to a lighter blue. While the wash for the sky is still wet, you should dab out the colour with a damp tissue or sponge for the clouds.

Use a damp tissue or paper towel to dab out the colour for the clouds.

3. Next add the background, gradually working forward to the near foreground areas. Rather than diluting, gradually add more and more of the new colour. Allow the colours to merge but allow one area to dry before moving to a new one, to avoid unwanted bleeding.

For the background, grade from one colour to another, adding colour to the edge to give shape while the wash is still damp.

23

Use a pale yellow to light brown wash to draw the track.

4. Use a pale wash to draw the track. Add colour to shape the edges, and dab off the colour in the middle of the track with a paper towel. Avoid filling the track with colour as it is better to give the impression of a lighter touch.

Add colour to the wash wet-in-wet to create this effect.

5. To create the green-blue effect in the background trees and shrubs, use the wet-in-wet technique. While the green foliage is still wet paint in the blue shading. The addition of this detail will help bring life to the foliage and to the painting as a whole.

Adding detail to foliage will help to give your work definition.

6. For the tree in the centre of the picture start with a green wash before adding more colour. When this is nearly dry, add the three darker colours. These will help to give shape and definition to the tree, one of the main focal points of the painting.

7. Where you wish to keep areas of the painting white, use masking fluid (available from art shops) for the task. Follow the manufacturer's instructions and once the fluid is dry, add a wash of the appropriate colour. When the light colour is dry add a darker colour. When this final colour is dry, remove the masking agent and paint over with the lightest colour if desired.

Use masking fluid to keep areas white. If necessary, this can be painted over later.

Detailed Landscape

Painting a more detailed landscape
offers a different challenge to a
simple one, but can turn out to
be more rewarding.

1. Begin by sketching or tracing the line drawing on page 59. The sketch opposite can be used to establish tonal values. Pencil in the main shapes, always considering where the light is coming from and where the highlights are to fall on your subject.

2. Wash in the sky areas with different shades of blue, leaving the areas of foliage white. If you like, use a liquid mask to keep the relevant areas white. When painting sky, start with the darkest blue before adding water to the pigment, so that the colour gradually fades to a lighter blue. When this is dry, add a pale green wash for the tree foliage.

When the pale green wash is dry, add more colour to shape the foliage, adding dark colour wet-in-wet.

3. For the grass, use the lightest colour first, adding progressively darker colours. Let each colour dry before adding the new one. Apply a wash to the tree trunk first. Let this dry, then add a light colour, gradually getting slightly darker. Let this dry, then add the darkest colour wet-in-wet in some areas for texture.

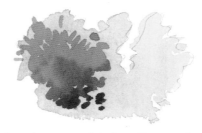

When the tree foliage is dry, work on the ground details. Put down the lightest colours in the foliage and foreground grass, path and tree trunks first.

27

For the house, only the roof should be painted wet-in-wet.

Use the wet-in-wet technique for the hills in the distance. In this instance, you will find it easier to scrape out white detail in the water with a knife rather than using a masking agent.

Use successive washes for the path. Varying the colour will help to make your picture more three-dimensional.

4. With the sky and greenery complete you can start work on the house and distant hills. Each distinct area of the house should be painted on dry paper except for the roof where the colour is washed on another colour wet-in-wet.

5. When the house is dry, the picture's tonal values will be fully established. Use wet-in-wet for the distant hills, adding some paler colour on top when the wash is nearly dry. The darker waves should be detailed first. When dry, add a pale wash on top. Scrape out white detail with a sharp knife.

6. Keep the path light with mottled colours, adding successive washes as soon as the previous colour has dried. When this is complete the only thing left to do is to work up the details until you are happy that the picture is finished.

Harbour Scene

Painting harbour scenes requires a greater knowledge of drawing. No-one is going to notice a misplaced branch on a tree but a boat mast must be painted at the right angle.

1. Sketch or trace the line drawing on page 63. Use the close-up sketch here to establish tonal values. Pencil in the main shapes, thinking about where the light is coming from and where the highlights will be in the painting.

2. Wash in the sky areas with different shades of blue. Start with the darkest blue before adding water to the pigment, so that the colour gradually fades to a lighter blue. As the cloud cover is more substantial in this project you should paint them using the wet-in-wet technique.

The cloud is established using the wet-in-wet technique.

3. As with the sky, add a graduated wash for the sea. Use different shades of blue starting with the darkest, then add water to the pigment to create lighter shades. When the wash is dry, add a brownish wash for the harbour walls before adding the detail to it.

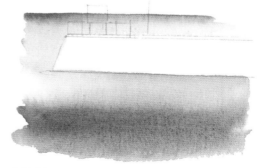

Add the wash for the harbour wall area before adding the detail.

Paint the shadows of the sea, covering the highlighted areas with masking fluid.

Use simple colours for the figure.

For the detail in all the boats, add the lighter colours before completing with the darker ones.

4. As with the harbour wall, add a simple wash for the foreground boat. The details can be added when this is dry. Also paint the shadows of the sea, covering the highlighted areas with masking fluid. The white areas around the boat will help to give it a sense of movement.

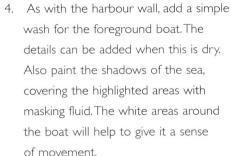

5. It is not necessary to go into a great deal of detail for the figures on the boat so use simple colours. Having said that, take care with skin tones or you run the risk of ruining the quality of the picture over a small point of interest.

6. For the detail of the boats in the background you should begin by adding the lighter colours first. Complete with the darker colours of the boats' windows and hulls when these are dry.

7. Add the details to the boat in the foreground last. Use a rigger brush for the lines of the boat as these are ideal for adding fine details. However, if you don't feel confident with a rigger brush, use a ruler instead. With the edge lifted, carefully run the brush along it to get straight lines.

Still Life

The advantage of painting still life is the degree of control it offers. You can control the lighting, the size, the shape and the colour of your object.

1. Sketch or trace the line drawing on page 60. Use the close-up sketch here to establish tonal values. Use a pencil for the main shapes, making sure you are aware of where the light is coming from and where the highlights will fall on your subject.

2. Flowers are created with a wash of the lightest colour. While this is wet, remove sections of paint for the lightest areas with a dry, clean brush. Use wet-in-wet to add darker colours, moulding the shape of the petals. When almost dry, add the detail of the darkest areas. For the tulips work on the yellow areas first. When this is nearly dry, add a pale version of the red so that the yellow and red blend together. Then add darker reds to mould the shape of the petals.

Use a wash of the lightest colour for the flowers. The wet-in-wet technique should be used to add darker colours, moulding the shape of the petals.

3. For the leaves, use a pale wash first. Lift off the colour for the lightest-coloured areas with a damp paper towel. When this is almost dry add the darker colour to shape the leaf.

When all the washes for the leaves are dry scrape off some of the colour with a sharp blade to reveal the textured highlights.

Use the wet-in-wet technique for the vase and bowl. Start with a light wash, adding darker washes to build up the shape.

The wet-in-wet technique is also used to shape the colours of the larger fruit.

Use a masking agent for the white highlights of the grapes and a pale green wash for the remainder.

4. In order to paint the vase and bowl, you should use the wet-in-wet technique. Start with a light wash, then remove some of the colour with a damp paper towel. Then add the darker washes wet-in-wet, gradually building up the shape of the vase. When this is dry, finish off the detail of the darker areas.

5. You should also use the wet-in-wet technique to shape the various colours of the larger fruit. Once again, begin with a light wash before adding the darker colours for the shadows. When dry, add the final details.

6. For the grapes, use a pale wash. Use a masking agent to reserve the white highlight. As always, it is this attention to detail that will improve the quality of your work. Add the slightly darker colour wet-in-wet and the final details when this is dry.

Drawing Animals

Drawing cats, dogs and horses in preparation for a painting is relatively simple as the same principles apply to all three.

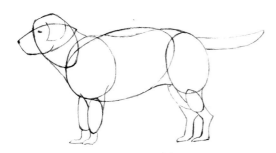

Dogs

The basic dog shape can be drawn using different-shaped ovals. Simply add long, thin ovals for the dog's legs, then use shading to add the coat.

Cats

To draw a cat or kitten, start with two circles and part of a circle for the chest. Add an oval for the back legs, then draw in sausage shapes for the front legs and ovals for the paws. Complete the cat or kitten by adding facial features and fur.

By changing the angles of your shapes, you can easily draw a playful kitten.

Horses

If you break it down into simple shapes, a horse is as simple to draw as a dog or cat.

Draw two bean shapes, one for the body, one for the neck, then two circles for the top of the front and back legs. Copy the leg and hoof shapes. Draw small circles for the leg joints, then a long oval for the head. Add circles at the top and bottom of the head, ears and a tail. Complete by adding facial details, mane and shading.

Practicality

Of course, the problem with painting animals is their tendency to move. One way to get round this is to paint from a photograph but this method also has its disadvantages. When painting animals you should strive to bring a sense of their vitality to your work and this is something likely to be lost in a photograph. Perhaps the best solution is to combine the two, sketching from life but painting from a photograph.

Horse

Horses are a wonderful subject for
animal lovers. A good painting
can bring out the essential
character of the animal.

1. Sketch or trace the line drawing on page 61. The close-up detail here can be used to establish tonal values. Use a pencil for the main shapes, making sure you give due consideration to where the light is coming from and where the highlights are to fall on your subject.

2. Although the horse's eye forms only a small proportion of the painting, getting it right is crucial to the quality of the finished picture. Paint the eye with a grey wash, reserving the white highlight. This should bring a dark grey/black shape to the eye.

The eye should be detailed with a grey wash. The white highlight should be reserved. Then use a light brown to fill the majority of the eye, then sweep a curving wash of dark brown in the eye, as shown.

3. For the colour of the horse's mane and ears, begin with a brown-red wash. While the wash is still wet, remove some of the paint with a dryish brush rinsed in clean water. This will lift off the colour, helping to bring vitality to the mane. Continue to build colour with different shades of brown.

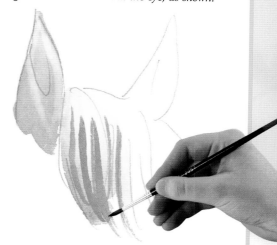

Use a dryish brush rinsed in clean water to lift off colour.

Start with a light wash for the horse's nose.

Create highlights by removing the wash while still wet with a paper towel.

After working the colour into the horse's mane, finish the impression of hair with a rigger brush.

4. Work in the opposite manner for the area around the horse's nose. Build up the colour with progressively darker colours – this will help you to create shape, giving definition to the nose.

5. Apply a light brown wash to the horse's body, then remove the areas you want to stay lighter with a paper towel. Add definition to the horse's form by applying progressively darker colours. Continue using a dabbing technique to leave a texture.

6. After working the colour into the horse's mane (Step 3), finish the impression of hair by adding a fine line with a rigger brush. Add a pale wash of colour to the background to finish.

Basic Anatomy

1. The line and dot technique is a simple method to draw the human form. Begin by drawing a stick figure. Draw a small dot at the point of each body joint.

2. Now draw a stick figure in an action pose. You will need to take into account the body's centre of gravity, which is typically located just above the crotch. The relationship of the centre of gravity to the body's 'resting points' will dictate the sense of movement.

3. The stick figure establishes the figure's proportions. Now join up the dots with cylinder shapes to give the figure its body. Note that the legs (at the waist) are roughly half the total height of the figure and that, with the arm hanging freely, the bottom of the hand comes about halfway down the thigh.

4. Smooth out the cylinder shapes to give the impression of muscles and clothing.

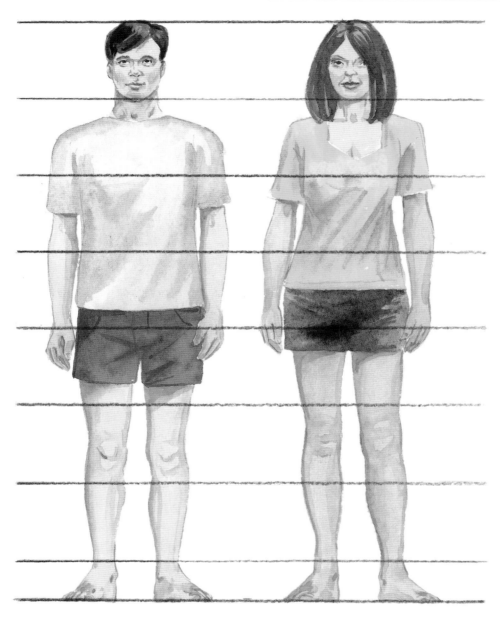

The human figure can be divided into six separate parts, all of similar proportions to one another apart from the feet division which is smaller.

Dividing the body up in this way will help you to keep the figure in correct proportion.

45

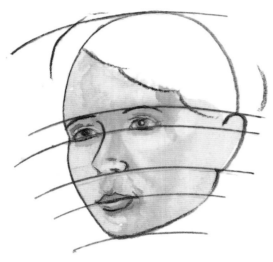

The distance from the nose line to the eyebrows and from the nose line to the bottom of the chin is roughly the same. The distance from the eye line to the bottom of the chin and from the eye line to the top of the head is roughly similar. The ear should extend from the nose line to the eyebrow line.

The Head

5. The head is usually approximately one-seventh the size of the body. However, bear in mind when drawing from life that body shape varies from person to person. The head will also be one-third the width of the shoulders. The proportions of the head itself are broken up into separate areas. The top of the head to the eyebrow line forms one part, the eyebrow line to below the nose another part and from the bottom of the nose to the chin another. There are two further subdivisions, the eyeline and the mouthline.

6. Not only should you use horizontal guidelines for the head you should use vertical ones as well. Two vertical lines drawn up from the lips should touch the inside of each iris. Vertical lines within the lip lines should mark out the width of the nose.

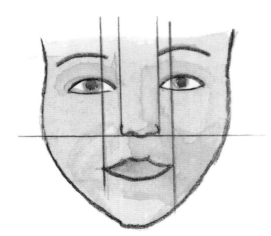

Use guidelines to position the lips and nose correctly.

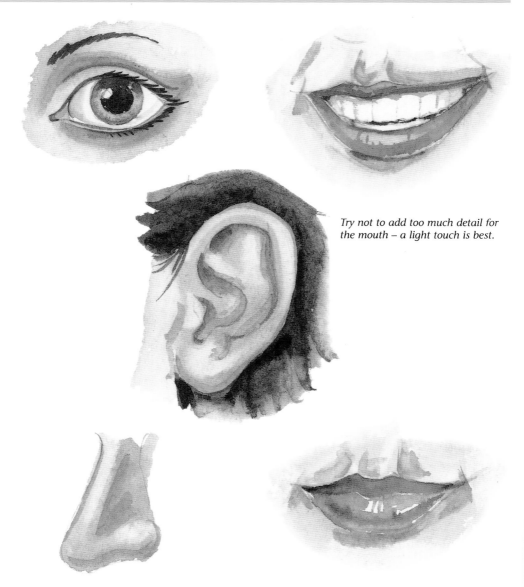

Try not to add too much detail for the mouth – a light touch is best.

Getting the shading correct is crucial for the eyes, nose and ears.

The top lip should be darker than the bottom lip.

47

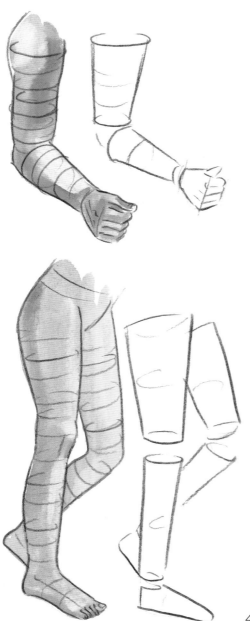

Arms and Legs

7. The arm is drawn in three cylinder shapes: the upper arm, the lower arm and the hand. The hand should be approximately one-third the length of the arm. When drawing arms in great detail it is worth remembering that there are three main bones: the radius, the ulna and the humerus.

8. You should approach the legs in the same way that you approach the other parts of the body, by breaking them down into simple geometric shapes. As with the arm, the leg should be divided into three cylindrical shapes, one for the upper leg, one for the lower leg and one for the foot. The key to success when drawing anatomical figures is always to break them down into more manageable shapes.

Hands and Feet

9. Hands and feet are notoriously difficult to draw but they needn't be. Draw a box-like shape to establish the foot's form and proportion. As with hands to arms, feet will be one-third the length of the legs. Although the head is divided into halves, most other proportions work in thirds.

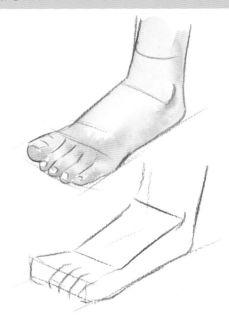

10. Smooth out the box shape to give detail to the foot.

11. Use the same technique for the hands. Draw a box-like shape to establish form and proportion, then smooth out the box shape to give detail. Never overwork the details of feet or hands as they can look laboured and draw away attention from what may be otherwise a good-quality painting. Treat them sympathetically but always keep them simple.

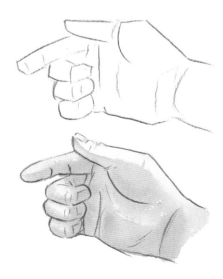

Life Study

A life study presents a different challenge
to other watercolour subjects. However, as
long as you are able to master the basics of
anatomy, it will not be too daunting a task.

1. Sketch or trace the line drawing on page 62. Use the sketch opposite to help you establish tonal values. Use a pencil for the main shapes, making sure you consider where the light is coming from and where the highlights will fall on your subject.

2. Cover the white of the bench with a masking agent. Apply a light greeny-yellow wash to the hedge and allow to dry.

Begin with a light greeny-yellow wash for the hedge.

3. Build up the colours of the hedge using the wet-in-wet technique. Allow to dry before adding concentrated blobs of colour to finish the hedge.

4. Apply a pale wash of creamy brown to the ground and work wet-in-wet to add darker colours. Leave to dry, then add the details of the stones.

This detail shows the build-up of colours on the hedge.

For the face, add a light wash on top of the pencil sketch.

Use a fine brush to add the details of the face.

The creases of the clothing should be established in the pencil drawing so that they can be washed over.

5. In order to paint the face and arms, begin by adding a very light brown wash on top of your pencil sketch. Then add more washes of different hues to build up the detail of the skin tone.

6. Use a fine brush to add the details of the face. Try to be precise when painting eyes, lips and teeth. Use a light brown wash for the hair, adding the darker highlights using the wet-in-wet technique. Do not labour detail or these areas will become muddy.

7. The creases of the clothing should be established in the pencil drawing. It is this sort of attention to detail that makes all the difference when painting life studies, as it makes the subject seem more real. Use a light blue-lilac wash for the T-shirt, washing in darker colour for the shadow.

8. Use a dark blue wash for the jeans, dabbing out the colour with a paper tissue. When this is dry add the final parts of the shoes, clothing and dark glasses. When this is complete, work up the details until you are happy that the picture is finished.

Add the detail of the shoes and clothing last.

Art Appreciation

Midsummer Eve – Edward R Hughes © Christie's Images Ltd 1995

Midsummer Eve, by Edward Hughes (1851–1914), painted in a mixture of watercolour and gouache, shows to good effect the artist's perfectionist tendencies. As you study this depiction of Titania, Queen of the Fairies, your eyes are inevitably drawn towards the fairies at the bottom of the picture and the extraordinary level of detail the artist has provided here.

Christmas Roses — WCD Dobson © Christie's Images Ltd 1994

Christmas Roses – William Dobson

The Harvest Moon – Helen Allingham © Christie's Images Ltd 2003

The Harvest Moon, 'Globed in Mellow Splendour' – Helen Allingham

Christmas Roses by William Dobson (1817–1898) is a fairly typical example of both the artist's strengths and weaknesses. The work's simplicity enables you to connect with it almost immediately but the posing of the model seems oversentimental. Intriguingly, Dobson was vehemently opposed to body colour, preferring to create an idealised notion of the human form.

Helen Allingham (1848–1926) is one of the few watercolour artists of the nineteenth century whose work remains popular today. The first woman to be elected a full member of The Royal Society of Watercolours, Allingham initially gained a reputation as a graphic designer, having provided illustrations for Thomas Hardy's novel, *Far From the Madding Crowd*.

The Harvest Moon, 'Globed in Mellow Splendour', depicting a rural scene with a large figure in the foreground, is typical of her early work. While the figure in the foreground seems disproportionate to the landscape this is to suggest man's mastery over the land. Playing with form is fraught with risk but in this case Allingham pulls it off.

Pharmakeutria – Marie Stillman © Christie's Images Ltd 1991

Marie Stillman (1844–1927) made a significant contribution to the Pre-Raphaelite movement, both as an artist and as a model. Renowned for her beauty, she posed for many of Dante Gabriel Rosetti's paintings. Like Edward Hughes, the sheer professionalism of her approach to painting shines through. As with all her pictures *Pharmakeutria* is detailed, highly accomplished and yet somehow there is a charming 'naive' flatness to the perspective.

Pharmakeutria (Brewing the Love Philtre) – Marie Stillman (née Spartali)

Grand Canal – JMW Turner © Christie's Images Ltd 1999

Joseph Mallord William Turner (1775–1851) is still regarded as one of England's greatest painters and one of the world's leading watercolourists.

The painting here is typical of much of Turner's work in watercolours. There is a Romantic element to his depiction of the Grand Canal, and this is to some degree achieved by his flooding of the landscape with a brilliant, hazy light.

The Grand Canal, Venice, with Gondolas and Figures in the Foreground – Joseph Mallord William Turner

Wharf at Ironbound – John Singer Sargent

John Singer Sargent became the most fashionable portrait painter in London in the 1880s. However, while his portraits made him a superstar in the art world his watercolour landscapes were also well received. These were heavily influenced by the Impressionists, whose aims were to depict real life, to paint straight from nature, and to capture the changing effects of light. *Wharf at Ironbound* eloquently displays two of the traits that made Sargent so distinguished an artist: his control of light and his complete mastery of perspective.

The Green Parasol – John Singer Sargent

It can be instructive to contrast two pictures by the same artist. While still an outdoor scene displaying an easy mastery of perspective and light *The Green Parasol* is full of humour. The picture appears to show a typical response to a hot sun – a desire to bathe in it – and yet perhaps Sargent wants us to read more into the work than what we can see on the surface. While the pair seem to be enjoying a sunny day perhaps the 'lady' in the foreground has had too much to drink – an idea suggested by her ungainly pose.

57

Drawings to Use

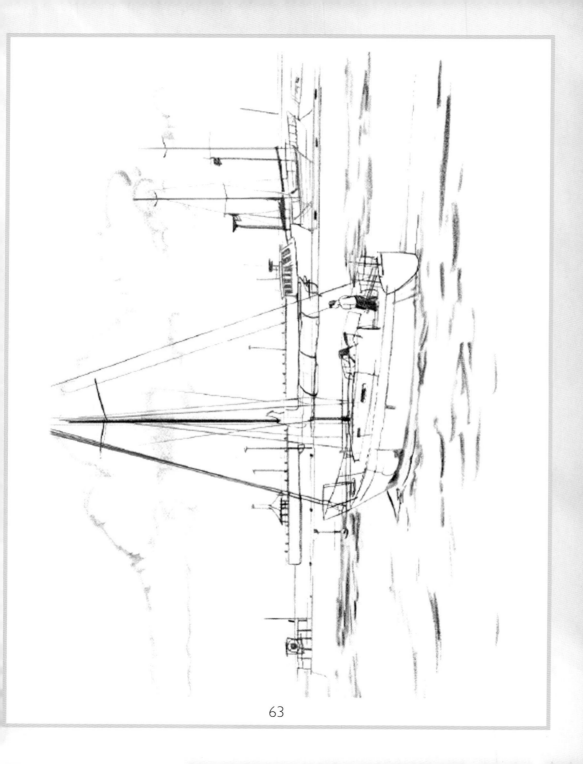

Conclusion

The advantage that watercolour painting has over other styles of painting is that, with practice and a keen eye, you can progress rapidly from novice to accomplished painter in a relatively short period of time. For the dedicated artist it should be a matter of months or even weeks before you can explore a variety of techniques.

Even so, it may take time before you discover the subject matter to which you are best suited. Will you be drawn to landscapes or will you prefer the precision of still life? The basic techniques covered in this book should give you the ability to develop your skills in either field.

When you feel confident in your ability, why not consider exhibiting your work? Of course, any creative work one undertakes is deeply personal but placing your work alongside others will allow you to take an objective view of how your skills are progressing. While you may be fearful of negative feedback there is also the possibility that your work will be appreciated for its quality. As long as the criticism is constructive you are sure to move forward with your work.